Introduction

Como is the Big Easy – a beautiful superchunky yarn that is perfect for the simple knits featured in this collection of 16 designs.

Como creates the soft knits that are just right for autumn, it's unstructured nature gives wonderful stitch definition to classic ribs, moss and stocking stitch and also makes even the most generously sized designs light and easy to wear.

Brioche gilet

Ribbed cape

Cricket jumper

Moss stitch and rib jacket

Simple cardigan

Moss stitch coat

T shape sweater

Mock rib jumper

Ribbed scarf

Reversible bag

Broken rib cardigan

Tank top

Striped sweater

Moss stitch scarf
& Daisy stitch hat

Contents

Basic information

The quantities of yarn are based on average requirements and are therefore approximate. It is essential to work to the stated tension and you should always knit a tension square before starting. If you have too many stitches to 10cm/4in your tension is tight and you should change to a larger needle. If there are too few stitches, your tension is loose and you should change to a smaller needle. We cannot accept responsibility for the finished product if any yarn other than the one specified is used. Instructions given are for the first size, with larger sizes in round brackets. Where only one figure or instruction is given this applies to all sizes.

Work all directions inside square brackets the number of times stated. See ball band for washing and pressing instructions.

STANDARD ABBREVIATIONS

alt = alternate
beg = beginning
cont = continue
dec = decrease
foll = following
inc = increase
k = knit
kfb = knit into front and back of st
m1 = make one st by picking up the loop lying between st just worked and next st and working into back of it
p = purl
pfb = purl into front and back of st
patt = pattern
psso = pass slipped st over
rem = remaining
rep = repeat
skpo = slip 1, knit 1, pass slipped stitch over
sl = slip
ssk = [sl 1 knitwise] twice, insert tip of left needle from left to right through front of both sts and k2tog
st(s) = stitch(es)
st st = stocking stitch
tbl = through back loop
tog = together
yf = yarn forward
yo = yarn over needle
yrn = yarn round needle
y2rn = yarn round needle twice to make 2 sts

USA GLOSSARY

cast off = bind off
moss stitch = seed stitch
tension = gauge
stocking stitch = stockinette stitch
yarn forward, yarn over needle, or yarn round needle = yarn over

Brioche gilet

Ribbed cape

Cricket jumper

Moss stitch and rib jacket

Simple cardigan

Shawl collared jacket

Moss stitch coat

T shape sweater

Mock rib jumper

Ribbed scarf

Reversible bag

Broken rib cardigan

Tank top

Striped sweater

Moss stitch scarf &
Daisy stitch hat

Brioche gilet

MEASUREMENTS

To fit bust

86–92	92–97	102–107	cm
34–36	36–38	40–42	in

FINISHED MEASUREMENTS

Bust

100	112	124	cm
39½	44	48¾	in

Length to back neck

58	60	62	cm
22¾	23½	24½	in

MATERIALS

• 14(16:18) 50g balls Debbie Bliss Como in Navy 08.
• Pair each 9mm (US 13) and 10mm (US 15) knitting needles.

TENSIONS

10 sts and 15 rows over st st and 9 sts and 20 rows over patt, both to 10cm/4in square using 10mm (US 15) needles.

ABBREVIATIONS

See page 22.

BRIOCHE STITCH

On the wrong side rows, bring the yarn to the front, slip the next st purlwise, then k the foll st, so making one st. On the following row, the slipped st and the made st are worked as k2tog.

BACK

With 9mm (US 13) needles, cast on 45(51:57) sts.
1st row (right side) K1, [p1, k1] to end.
2nd row P1, [k1, p1] to end.
Rep the last 2 rows 4 times more and the 1st row again, increasing one st at centre of last row. 46(52:58) sts.
Change to 10mm (US 15) needles.
1st row (wrong side) K1, [yf, sl 1, k1] to last st, k1.
2nd row K2, [k2tog, k1] to end.
3rd row K2, [yf, sl 1, k1] to end.
4th row [K1, k2tog] to last 2 sts, k2.
These 4 rows **form** the patt and are repeated throughout.

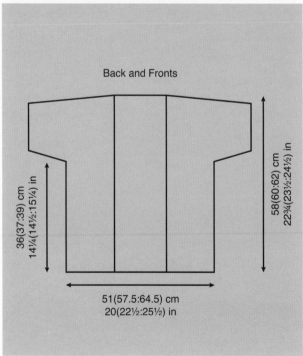

Back and Fronts

36(37:39) cm
14¼(14½:15¼) in

58(60:62) cm
22¾(23½:24½) in

51(57.5:64.5) cm
20(22½:25½) in

Cont in patt until back measures 36(37:39)cm/
14¼(14½:15¼)in from beg, ending with a wrong side row.
Shape sleeves
Cast on 4 sts at beg of next 6 rows. 70(76:82) sts.
Cont in patt until back measures 53(55:57)cm/
21(21¾:22½)in from beg, ending with a wrong side row.
Shape shoulders
Cast off 6 sts at beg of next 6 rows and 5(6:7) sts
at beg of foll 4 rows.
Cast off rem 14(16:18) sts.

LEFT FRONT

With 9mm (US 13) needles, cast on 15(17:19) sts.
1st row (right side) P1, [k1, p1] to end.
2nd row K1, [p1, k1] to end.
Rep the last 2 rows 4 times more and the 1st row again,
increasing one st at centre of last row. 16(18:20) sts.
Change to 10mm (US 15) needles.
1st row (wrong side) K1, [yf, sl 1, k1] to last st, k1.
2nd row K2, [k2tog, k1] to end.
3rd row K2, [yf, sl 1, k1] to end.
4th row [K1, k2tog] to last 2 sts, k2.
These 4 rows **form** the patt and are repeated throughout.
Cont in patt until back measures 36(37:39)cm/
14¼(14½:15¼)in from beg, ending with a wrong side row.
Shape sleeve
Cast on 4 sts at beg of next row and 2 foll right side rows.
28(30:32) sts.
Cont in patt until front measures same as Back
to shoulder, ending at sleeve edge.
Shape shoulder
Cast off 6 sts at beg of next and 2 foll right side rows.
Work 1 row.
Cast off 5(6:7) sts at beg of next row.
Work 1 row.
Cast off rem 5(6:7) sts.

RIGHT FRONT

With 9mm (US 13) needles, cast on 15(17:19) sts.
1st row (right side) P1, [k1, p1] to end.
2nd row K1, [p1, k1] to end.
Rep the last 2 rows 4 times more and the 1st row again,
increasing one st at centre of last row. 16(18:20) sts.
Change to 10mm (US 15) needles.
1st row (wrong side) K1, [yf, sl 1, k1] to last st, k1.
2nd row K2, [k2tog, k1] to end.
3rd row K2, [yf, sl 1, k1] to end.
4th row [K1, k2tog] to last 2 sts, k2.

These 4 rows **form** the patt and are repeated throughout.
Cont in patt until back measures 36(37:39)cm/
14¼(14½:15¼)in from beg, ending with a right side row.
Shape sleeve
Cast on 4 sts at beg of next row and 2 foll wrong side rows.
28(30:32) sts.
Cont in patt until front measures same as Back to shoulder,
ending at sleeve edge.
Shape shoulder
Cast off 6 sts at beg of next and 2 foll wrong side rows.
Work 1 row.
Cast off 5(6:7) sts at beg of next row.
Work 1 row.
Cast off rem 5(6:7) sts.

RIGHT FRONT BAND

Join shoulder and upper arm seams.
Place a marker at centre back neck.
With right side facing and 9mm (US 13) needles,
pick up and k63(64:65) sts evenly along right front edge
to shoulder, 6(7:8) sts across back to marker, turn
and cast on one st. 70(72:74) sts.
Rib row [K1, p1] to end.
Rep the last row until band measures 12(13:14)cm/
4¾(5:5½)in, ending with a wrong side row.
Cast off in rib.

LEFT FRONT BAND

With right side facing and 9mm (US 13) needles,
cast on one st, pick up and k6(7:8) sts across back neck
from marker to shoulder and 63(64:65) sts evenly along
left front to cast on edge. 70(72:74) sts.
Rib row [K1, p1] to end.
Rep the last row until band measures 12(13:14)cm/
4¾(5:5½)in, ending with a wrong side row. Cast off in rib.

ARMBANDS

With right side facing and 9mm (US 13) needles,
pick up and k48(52:56) sts evenly around armhole edge.
Rib row [K1, p1] to end.
Rep the last row until band measures 5cm/2in,
ending with a wrong side row.
Cast off in rib.

TO MAKE UP

Join side and armband seams. Join row ends
of front bands at centre back.

Ribbed cape

MEASUREMENTS

To fit bust

81–86	92–97	102–107	112–117	cm
32–34	36–38	40–42	44–46	in

FINISHED MEASUREMENTS

Width at lower edge

70	75	80	85	cm
27½	29½	31½	33½	in

Length to shoulder

30cm/12in for all sizes

MATERIALS

- 11(12:12:13) 50g balls Debbie Bliss Como in Denim 007.
- 9mm (US 13) and 10mm (US 15) circular needles.

TENSION

10 sts and 15 rows to 10cm/4in square over 2 x 2 rib using 10mm (US 15) needles.

ABBREVIATIONS

See page 22.

RIGHT FRONT AND BACK

With 10mm (US 15) circular needle, cast on 100(107:114:121) sts.
Work backwards and forwards in rows as follows:
1st row (right side) K7, p2, [k5, p2] to end.
2nd row K2, [p5, k2] to end.
These 2 rows **form** the rib with garter st edging.
Cont in patt until work measures 9cm/3½in from cast on edge, ending with a wrong side row.
Dec row K4, skpo, k1, p2, [k1, skpo, k2, p2] to end.
86(92:98:104) sts.
Next row K2, [p4, k2] to end.
Cont in patt until work measures 16cm/6¼in from cast on edge, ending with a wrong side row.
Dec row K3, skpo, k1, p2, [k1, skpo, k1, p2] to end.
72(77:82:87) sts.
Next row K2, [p3, k2] to end.
Cont in patt until work measures 23cm/9in from cast on edge, ending with a wrong side row.
Dec row K2, skpo, k1, p2, [k1, skpo, p2] to end.
58(62:66:70) sts.

70(75:80:85) cm
27½(29½:31½:33½) in

30 cm/12 in

Next row K2, [p2, k2] to end.
Cont in patt until work measures 30cm/12in from
cast on edge, ending with a wrong side row.
Dec row K2, [skpo, p2] to end. 44(47:50:53) sts.
Next row K2, [p1, k2] to end.
Leave these sts on a spare needle

LEFT FRONT AND BACK

With 10mm (US 15) circular needle, cast on
100(107:114:121) sts.
Work backwards and forwards in rows as follows:
1st row (right side) P2, [k5, p2] to last 7 sts, k7.
2nd row K2, [p5, k2] to end.
These 2 rows **form** the rib with garter st edging.
Cont in patt until work measures 9cm/3½in from
cast on edge, ending with a wrong side row.
Dec row P2, [k1, skpo, k2, p2] to last 7 sts,
k1, skpo, k4. 86(92:98:104) sts.
Next row K2, [p4, k2] to end.
Cont in patt until work measures 16cm/6¼in from
cast on edge, ending with a wrong side row.
Dec row P2, [k1, skpo, k1, p2] to last 6 sts,
k1, skpo, k3. 72(77:82:87) sts.
Next row K2, [p3, k2] to end.
Cont in patt until work measures 23cm/9in from
cast on edge, ending with a wrong side row.
Dec row P2, [k1, skpo, p2] to last 5 sts,
k1, skpo, k2. 58(62:66:70) sts.
Next row K2, [p2, k2] to end.
Cont in patt until work measures 30cm/12in from
cast on edge, ending with a wrong side row.
Dec row P2, [skpo, p2] to last 4 sts, skpo, k2.
44(47:50:53) sts.
Next row K2, [p1, k2] to end.

COLLAR

With right side facing and 9mm (US 13) circular needle,
rib 30(33:36:39) sts of left front and back, place wrong side
of right front over right side of left front and back,
[rib next st of right front and next st of left front tog]
14 times, rib across rem 30(33:36:39) sts of right front
and back. 74(80:86:92) sts.

Work backwards and forwards in rows as follows:
Next row (wrong side) K2, [p1, k2] to end.
Next row P2, [k1, p2] to end.
Rep the last 2 rows for 10cm/4in, ending with a right side row.
Next row (wrong side) K2, [p1, m1, k2] to end.
98(106:114:122) sts.
Next row P2, [k2, p2] to end.
Cont in rib for a further 5cm/2in.
Change to 10mm (US 15) needles.
Cont in rib for a further 15cm/6in.
Cast off in rib.

TO MAKE UP

Join back seam, reversing seam on collar.

Cricket jumper

MEASUREMENTS

To fit chest

92–97	102–107	112–117 cm
36–38	40–42	44–46 in

FINISHED MEASUREMENTS

Chest

120	132	144 cm
47¼	52	56¾ in

Length to shoulder

63	64	65 cm
24¾	25¼	25½ in

Sleeve length

48cm/19in for all sizes

MATERIALS

- 16(18:20) 50g balls Debbie Bliss Como in Rust 14 (M),
  1(2:2) 50g balls in Ecru 03 (A) and one 50g ball
  in Blue 06 (B).
- Pair each 9mm (US 13) and 10mm (US 15) needles.

TENSION

10 sts and 15 rows to 10cm/4in square over st st
using 10mm (US 15) needles.

ABBREVIATIONS

See page 22.

BACK

With 10mm (US 15) needles and M, cast on 62(68:74) sts.
1st row [P1, k1] to end.
This row **forms** the rib.
Rib a further 9 rows and inc one st at centre of last row.
63(69:75) sts.
Beg with a k row, work in st st stripes of 2 rows M,
1 row A, 1 row M and 1 row B, then cont in M only
until 82(84:86) rows have been worked in st st.
Shape shoulders
Cast off 19(21:23) sts at beg of next 2 rows.
Leave rem 25(27:29) sts. on a holder.

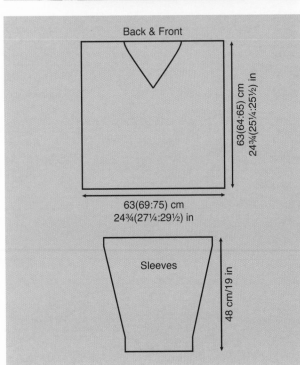

Back & Front

63(64:65) cm
24¾(25¼:25½) in

63(69:75) cm
24¾(27¼:29½) in

Sleeves

48 cm/19 in

FRONT

Work as given for Back until 54 rows have been worked.
Shape neck
Next row K27(30:33), k2tog, k2, turn and work on
these sts only for first side of neck shaping.
Work 1 row.
Next row K to last 4 sts, k2tog, k2.
Next row P to end.
Rep the last 2 rows 10(11:12) times more. 19(21:23) sts.
Work 4 more rows.
Cast off.
With right side facing, slip centre st onto a safety-pin,
rejoin yarn to rem sts, k2, skpo, k to end.
Complete to match first side, reversing shaping.

SLEEVES

With 9mm (US 13) needles and M, cast on 30(34:38) sts.
Work 10 rows in rib as given for Back.
Change to 10mm (US 15) needles.
Beg with a k row, work in st st stripes of 2 rows M,
1 row A, 1 row M and 1 row B, then cont in M only.
P 1 row.
Inc row K3, m1, k to last 3 sts, m1, k3.
Work 5 rows.
Rep the last 6 rows 7 times and the inc row again.
48(52:56) sts.
Work 7 rows.
Cast off.

NECKBAND

Join right shoulder seam.
With right side facing, 9mm (US 13) needles and A,
pick up and k28(30:32) sts down left side of front neck,
k1 from centre front holder, pick up and k28(30:32) sts
up right side of front neck, k across 25(27:29) sts
from back neck holder. 82(88:94) sts.
1st row (wrong side) [K1, p1] to end.
This row **forms** and **sets** the rib.
Next row Rib 26(28:30), p2tog, k1, p2tog; rib to end.
Next row Rib to end.
Next row Rib 25(27:29), p2tog, k1, p2tog; rib to end.
Next row Rib to end.
Next row With M, rib 24(26:28), p2tog, k1, p2tog; rib to end.

Next row With B, rib to end.
Next row With B, rib 23(25:27), p2tog, k1, p2tog; rib to end.
Next row With B, rib to end.
Next row With B, rib 22(24:26), p2tog, k1, p2tog; rib to end.
Next row With M, rib to end.
With M, cast off in rib, decreasing at centre front
on this row as set.

TO MAKE UP

Join left shoulder and neckband seam. With centre
of cast off edge sleeve to shoulder, sew on sleeves.
Join side and sleeve seams.

Moss stitch and rib jacket

MEASUREMENTS

To fit bust

86–91	91–97	97–102	cm
34–36	36–38	38–40	in

FINISHED MEASUREMENTS

Bust

112	126	140	cm
44	49½	55	in

Length

68	70	72	cm
26¾	27½	28¼	in

Sleeve length

43cm/17in for all sizes

MATERIALS

- 21(23:25) 50g balls of Debbie Bliss Como in Ecru 03.
- Pair 10mm (US 15) knitting needles.
- Long 9mm (US 13) circular needle.

TENSION

9 sts and 18 rows to 10cm/4in square over moss st using 10mm (US 15) needles.

ABBREVIATIONS

See page 22.

NOTE

The sleeve increases are staggered, working into the first st of every 5th row to avoid excess bulk when joining the sleeve seam.

BACK

With 10mm (US 15) needles, cast on 53(59:65) sts.
Moss st row K1, [p1, k1] to end.
This row **forms** moss st and is repeated throughout.
Cont in moss st until back measures 46(47:48)cm/
18(18½:19)in from cast on edge, ending with a wrong side row.
Shape armholes
Cast off 6(7:8) sts at beg of next 2 rows. 41(45:49) sts.
Work straight until back measures 68(70:72)cm/
26¾(27½:28¼)in from cast on edge, ending with
a wrong side row.

Back & Fronts

46(47:48) cm
18(18½:19) in

68(70:72) cm
26¾(27½:28¼) in

59(65.5:72) cm
23¼(25¾:28¼) in

Sleeves

43 cm/17 in

Shape shoulders

Cast off 6(7:7) sts at beg of next 2 rows and 7(7:8) sts at beg of foll 2 rows.
Cast off rem 15(17:19) sts.

POCKET LININGS

(Make 2)
With 10mm (US 15) needles, cast on 9(11:13) sts.
Work 29 rows in moss st.
Leave sts on a holder.

LEFT FRONT

With 10mm (US 15) needles, cast on 19(21:23) sts.
Moss st row P1, [k1, p1] to end.
This row **forms** moss st and is repeated throughout.
Work a further 33 rows.
Place pocket
Next row (right side) Moss st 5, cast off next
9(11:13) sts, moss st to end.
Next row Moss st 5, patt across sts of one
pocket lining, moss st 5 sts.
Cont in moss st until front measures 46(47:48)cm/
18(18½:19)in from cast on edge, ending at side edge.
Shape armhole
Cast off 6(7:8) sts at beg of next row. 13(14:15) sts.
Cont in moss st until front measures same as Back
to shoulder, ending at armhole edge.
Shape shoulder
Cast off 6(7:7) sts at beg of next row.
Work 1 row.
Cast off rem 7(7:8) sts.

RIGHT FRONT

With 10mm (US 15) needles, cast on 19(21:23) sts.
Moss st row P1, [k1, p1] to end.
This row **forms** moss st and is repeated throughout.
Work a further 33 rows.
Place pocket
Next row (right side) Moss st 5, cast off next
9(11:13) sts, moss st to end.
Next row Moss st 5, patt across sts of rem
pocket lining, moss st 5 sts.
Cont in moss st until front measures 46(47:48)cm/
18(18½:19)in from cast on edge, ending at side edge.
Shape armhole
Cast off 6(7:8) sts at beg of next row. 13(14:15) sts.
Cont in moss st until front measures same as Back

to shoulder, ending at armhole edge.
Shape shoulder
Cast off 6(7:7) sts at beg of next row.
Work 1 row.
Cast off rem 7(7:8) sts.

SLEEVES

With 10mm (US 15) needles, cast on 27(31:35) sts.
Moss st row P1, [k1, p1] to end.
This row **forms** moss st and is repeated throughout.
Work 10 rows.
Inc row Inc in first st, moss st to end.
Work 4 rows.
Rep the last 5 rows until there are 39(43:47) sts.
Cont straight until sleeve measures 43cm/17in from
cast on edge, ending with a wrong side row.
Place markers at each end of last row.
Work a further 10(12:12) rows.
Cast off.

FRONT BAND

Join shoulder seams.
With right side facing and 9mm (US 13) circular needle,
pick up and k68(73:76) sts evenly along right front edge
to shoulder, 18(20:22) sts across back neck and 68(73:76)
sts down left front to cast on edge. 154(166:174) sts.
Work backwards and forwards in rows.
1st row P2, [k2, p2] to end.
2nd row K2, [p2, k2] to end.
Rep the last 2 rows 10(11:12) times more.
Cast off in rib.

TO MAKE UP

Sew sleeves into armholes easing to fit and with row ends
above markers sewn to sts cast off at underarm. Join side
and sleeve seams. Slipstitch pocket linings in place.

Simple cardigan

MEASUREMENTS

To fit bust

81–86	86–92	92–97	97–102	102–107	cm
32–34	34–36	36–38	38–40	40–42	in

FINISHED MEASUREMENTS

Bust

90	98	106	114	122	cm
35½	38½	41¾	44¾	48	in

Length to shoulder

44	46	49	52	54	cm
17¼	18	19¼	20½	21¼	in

Sleeve length

25	26	27	28	29	cm
10	10¼	10½	11	11½	in

MATERIALS

- 10(11:13:14:16) 50g balls of Debbie Bliss Como in Pale Green 05.
- Pair each 9mm (US 13) and 10mm (US 15) needles.
- 10mm (US 15) circular needle.
- One large button.

TENSION

10 sts and 15 rows to 10cm/4in square over st st using 10mm (US 15) needles.

ABBREVIATIONS

See page 22.

BACK

With 9mm (US 13) needles, cast on 55(59:63:67:71) sts.
K 5 rows.
Change to 10mm (US 15) needles.
Beg with a k row, work in st st.
Work 2(4:6:6:8) rows.
Dec row K4, skpo, k to last 6 sts, k2tog, k4.
Work 7 rows.
Rep the last 8 rows twice more and the dec row again.
47(51:55:59:63) sts.
Work straight until back measures 25(26:27:28:29)cm/
10(10¼:10¾:11:11½)in from cast on edge, ending with a p row.
Shape armholes
Cast off 4(4:5:5:6) sts at beg of next 2 rows.
Leave the rem 39(43:45:49:51) sts on a spare needle.

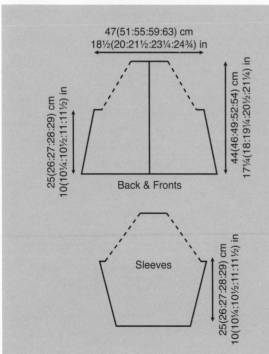

47(51:55:59:63) cm
18½(20:21½:23¼:24¾) in

44(46:49:52:54) cm
17¼(18:19¼:20½:21¼) in

25(26:27:28:29) cm
10(10¼:10½:11:11½) in

Back & Fronts

25(26:27:28:29) cm
10(10¼:10½:11:11½) in

Sleeves

LEFT FRONT

With 9mm (US 13) needles, cast on 29(31:33:35:37) sts.
K 5 rows.
Change to 10mm (US 15) needles.
Next row K to end.
Next row K2, p to end.
These 2 rows **form** st st with garter st edging.
Work a further 0(2:4:4:6) rows.
Dec row K4, skpo, k to end.
Work 7 rows.
Rep the last 8 rows twice more and the dec row again.
25(27:29:31:33) sts.
Work straight until front measures 25(26:27:28:29)cm/
10(10¼:10¾:11:11½)in from cast on edge, ending
with a wrong side row.
Shape armhole
Cast off 4(4:5:5:6) sts at beg of next row.
Work 1 row.
Leave the rem 21(23:24:26:27) sts on a spare needle.

RIGHT FRONT

With 9mm (US 13) needles, cast on 29(31:33:35:37) sts.
K 5 rows.
Change to 10mm (US 15) needles.
Next row K to end.
Next row P to last 2 sts, k2.
These 2 rows **form** st st with garter st edging.
Work a further 0(2:4:4:6) rows.
Dec row K to last 6 sts, k2tog, k4.
Work 7 rows.
Rep the last 8 rows twice more and the dec row again.
25(27:29:31:33) sts.
Work straight until front measures 25(26:27:28:29)cm/
10(10¼:10¾:11:11½)in from cast on edge, ending
with a right side row.
Shape armhole
Cast off 4(4:5:5:6) sts at beg of next row.
Leave the rem 21(23:24:26:27) sts on a spare needle.
Do not break yarn.

SLEEVES

With 9mm (US 13) needles, cast on 30(32:34:36:38) sts.
K 5 rows.
Change to 10mm (US 15) needles.
Beg with a k row, work in st st.
Work 4 rows.
Inc row K3, m1, k to last 3 sts, m1, k3.

Work 3 rows in st st.
Rep the last 4 rows 5(5:6:6:7) times more and the
inc row again. 44(46:50:52:56) sts.
Cont straight until sleeve measures 25(26:27:28:29)cm/
10(10¼:10¾:11:11½)in from cast on edge,
ending with a p row.
Shape top
Cast off 4(4:5:5:6) sts at beg of next 2 rows.
Leave rem 36(38:40:42:44) sts on a holder.

YOKE

With right side facing and 10mm (US 15) circular needle,
work across right front, right sleeve, back, left sleeve, and
left front as follows: k20(22:23:25:26) sts from right front,
k last st tog with first st of sleeve, k34(36:38:40:42), k last
st tog with first st of back, k37(41:43:47:49), k last st tog
with first st of sleeve, k34(36:38:40:42), k last st tog with first
st of left front, k20(22:23:25:26). 149(161:169:181:189) sts.
Work backwards and forwards in rows.
Next row (wrong side) K2, p to last 2 sts, k2.
Next row K19(21:22:24:25), p3tog, k32(34:36:38:40),
p3tog, k35(39:41:45:47), p3tog, k32(34:36:38:40),
p3tog, k19(21:22:24:25). 141(153:161:173:181) sts.
Next row K2, p to last 2 sts, k2.
Next row K18(20:21:23:24), p3tog, k30(32:34:36:38),
p3tog, k33(37:39:43:45), p3tog, k30(32:34:36:38),
p3tog, k18(20:21:23:24). 133(145:153:165:173) sts.
Next row K2, p to last 2 sts, k2.
Next row K17(19:20:22:23), p3tog, k28(30:32:34:36),
p3tog, k31(35:37:41:43), p3tog, k28(30:32:34:36),
p3tog, k17(19:20:22:23). 125(137:145:157:165) sts.
Next row K2, p to last 2 sts, k2.
Cont in this way dec 8 sts on next row and 3(4:5:6:7)
foll right side rows. 93(97:97:101:101) sts.
Next row K2, p to last 2 sts, k2.
Buttonhole row K2, k2tog, y2rn, skpo, k to end,
decreasing as set. 85(89:89:93:93) sts.
Next row Work to end, working twice in y2rn.
Change to 9mm (US 13) needles.
Next row K to end, decreasing as set.
Next row K to end.
Rep the last 2 rows once more and the first row again.
Cast off.

TO MAKE UP

Join side and sleeve seams. Join underarm seam.
Sew on button.

Shawl collared jacket

MEASUREMENTS

To fit bust

81–86	92–97	102–107	cm
32–34	36–38	40–42	in

FINISHED MEASUREMENTS

Bust

120	130	140	cm
47¼	51¼	55¼	in

Length to shoulder

60	62	64	cm
23½	24½	25½	in

Sleeve length

43	44	45	cm
17	17¼	17¾	in

MATERIALS

- 10(12:14) 50g balls of Debbie Bliss Como in Rust 14.
- Pair each 9mm (US 13) and 10mm (US 15) knitting needles.
- 3 buttons.

TENSION

10 sts and 15 rows to 10cm/4in square over st st using 10mm (US 15) needles.

ABBREVIATIONS

See page 22.

BACK

With 9mm (US 13) needles, cast on 62(67:72) sts.
K 9 rows.
Change to 10mm (US 15) needles.
Beg with a k row, work in st st until back measures 39(40:41)cm/15¼(15¾:16¼)in from cast on edge, ending with a p row.
Shape armholes
Cast off 5 sts at beg of next 2 rows. 52(57:62) sts.
Next row K2, skpo, k to last 4 sts, k2tog, k2.
Next row P to end.
Rep the last 2 rows 3(4:5) times more. 44(47:50) sts.
Cont straight until back measures 60(62:64)cm/23½(24½:25½)in from cast on edge, ending with a p row.

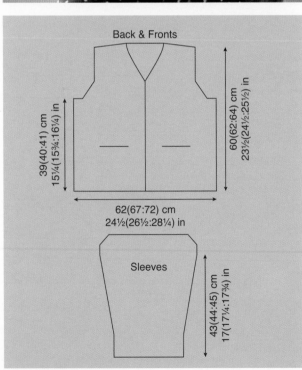

Back & Fronts

39(40:41) cm
15¼(15¾:16¼) in

60(62:64) cm
23½(24½:25½) in

62(67:72) cm
24½(26½:28¼) in

Sleeves

43(44:45) cm
17(17¼:17¾) in

Shape shoulders

Cast off 7(7:8) sts at beg of next 2 rows and 7(8:8) sts at beg of foll 2 rows. 16(17:18) sts.
Cast off.
Place a marker at centre of back neck edge.

POCKET LININGS

(Make 2)
With 10mm (US 15) needles, cast on 13(14:15) sts.
Beg with a k row, work 18(20:22) rows in st st.
Leave sts on a holder.

LEFT FRONT

With 9mm (US 13) needles cast on 34(37:40) sts.
K 9 rows.
Change to 10mm (US 15) needles.
Next row (right side) K to end.
Next row K8, p to end.
These 2 rows **form** st st with garter st front border.
Cont straight until front measures 17(18:19)cm/6¾(7:7½)in from cast on edge, ending with a wrong side row.
Place pocket
Next row K8(9:10), slip next 13(14:15) sts onto a holder, k across 13(14:15) sts of 1st pocket lining, k to end.
Cont straight until front measures 39(40:41)cm/ 15¼(15¾:16¼)in from cast on edge, ending with a wrong side row.
Shape armhole
Next row Cast off 5 sts, k to end. 29(32:35) sts.
Next row K8, p to end.
Next row K2, skpo, k to end.
Next row K8, p to end.
Rep the last 2 rows 3(4:5) times more. 25(27:29) sts.
Shape neck
Next row (right side) K to last 8 sts, slip these 8 sts onto a holder, turn and p to end.
Dec one st at neck edge on every foll 4th row until 14(15:16) sts rem.
Cont straight until front measures same as Back to shoulder, ending at armhole edge.
Shape shoulder
Next row Cast off 7(7:8) sts, patt to end.
Work 1 row.
Cast off rem 7(8:8) sts.
Mark position for 3 buttons, 3cm/1¼in, 13cm/5in and 23cm/9in down from start of neck shaping.

RIGHT FRONT

Work buttonholes to match markers as follows:
Buttonhole row (right side) K3, k2tog, yf, k to end.
With 9mm (US 13) needles, cast on 34(37:40) sts.
K 9 rows.
Change to 10mm (US 15) needles.
Next row (right side) K to end.
Next row P to last 8 sts, k8.
These 2 rows **form** st st with garter st front border.
Cont straight until front measures 17(18:19)cm/ 6¾(7:7½)in from cast on edge, ending with a wrong side row.
Place pocket
Next row K13(14:15), slip next 13(14:15) sts onto a holder, k across 13(14:15) sts of 2nd pocket lining, k to end.
Cont straight until front measures 39(40:41)cm/ 15¼(15¾:16¼)in from cast on edge, ending with a right side row.
Shape armhole
Next row Cast off 5 sts, p to last 8 sts, k8. 29(32:35) sts.
Next row K to last 4 sts, k2tog, k2.
Next row P to last 8 sts, k8.
Rep the last 2 rows 3(4:5) times more. 25(27:29) sts.
Shape neck
Next row (right side) K7, inc in next st, leave these 9 sts on a holder, k to end.
Dec one st at neck edge on every foll 4th row until 14(15:16) sts rem.
Cont straight until front measures same as Back to shoulder, ending at armhole edge.
Shape shoulder
Next row Cast off 7(7:8) sts, patt to end.
Work 1 row.
Cast off rem 7(8:8) sts.

SLEEVES

With 9mm (US 13) needles, cast on 30(34:38) sts.
K 9 rows.
Change to 10mm (US 15) needles.
Beg with a k row, work in st st.
Work 6 rows.
Inc row K5, m1, k to last 5 sts, m1, k5.
Work 7 rows.
Rep the last 8 rows 4 times more and the inc row again. 42(46:50) sts.
Cont straight until sleeve measures 43(44:45)cm/ 17(17¼:17¾)in from cast on edge, ending with a p row.
Place markers at each end of last row.

Work a further 6 rows.

Shape sleeve top

Next row K2, skpo, k to last 4 sts, k2tog, k2.

Next row P to end.

Rep the last 2 rows 3(4:5) times more. 34(36:38) sts.
Cast off.

LEFT COLLAR

With right side of left front facing and 9mm (US 13) needles,
inc in first st on holder, then k rem 7 sts of left front band. 9 sts.
K 1 row.

Cont in garter st, **at the same time,** inc one st at each end
of the next row and every foll 4th row until there are 19 sts,
ending wrong side of jacket and right side of collar facing.

Shape collar

** **Next 2 rows** K11, sl 1, turn and k to end.

K 4 rows **.

Rep from ** to ** until short edge of collar fits up left side
of front neck and across back neck to marker.
Cast off.

RIGHT COLLAR

With wrong side of right front facing and 9mm (US 13)
needles k across 9 sts on right front holder.

Cont in garter st, **at the same time,** inc one st at each end
of the next row and every foll 4th row until there are 19 sts.
K 1 row, so ending with right side of jacket and wrong side
of collar facing.

Shape collar

** **Next 2 rows** K11, sl 1, turn and k to end.

K 4 rows **.

Rep from ** to ** until short edge of collar fits up right
side of front neck and across back neck to marker.
Cast off.

POCKET TOPS

With right side facing and 9mm (US 13) needles,
k across 13(14:15) sts of first pocket.
K 6 rows.
Cast off.
Rep for second pocket.

TO MAKE UP

Join cast off edges of collar. Sew collar to neck edge.
Sew sleeves into armholes, easing to fit and with
row ends above markers sewn to sts cast off at underarm.
Join side and sleeve seams. Sew on buttons. Slipstitch
pocket linings and edges of pocket tops in place.

Moss stitch coat

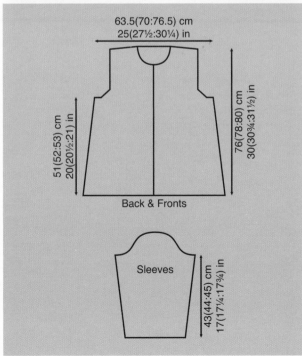

63.5(70:76.5) cm
25(27½:30¼) in

51(52:53) cm
20(20½:21) in

76(78:80) cm
30(30¾:31½) in

Back & Fronts

Sleeves

43(44:45) cm
17(17¼:17¾) in

MEASUREMENTS

To fit bust

81–86	92–97	102–107 cm
32–34	36–38	40–42 in

FINISHED MEASUREMENTS

Bust

117	131	145 cm
46	51¾	57 in

Length to shoulder

76	78	80 cm
30	30¾	31½ in

Sleeve length

43	44	45 cm
17	17¼	17¾ in

MATERIALS

- 24(26:28) 50g balls of Debbie Bliss Como in Red 12.
- Pair each 9 mm (US 13) and 10mm (US 15) knitting needles.
- One button.

TENSION

9 sts and 18 rows to 10cm/4in square over moss st using 10mm (US 15) needles.

ABBREVIATIONS

See page 22.

NOTE

The sleeve increases are staggered, working into the first st of every 7th row to avoid excess bulk when joining the sleeve seam.

BACK

With 9mm (US 13) needles, cast on 69(75:81) sts.
K 5 rows.
Change to 10mm (US 15) needles.
Moss st row (right side) K1, [p1, k1] to end.
Work a further 17(19:21) rows in moss st.
Dec row (right side) Moss st 8, k3tog, moss st to last 11 sts, k3tog, moss st 8.
Work 29 rows in moss st.

Rep the last 30 rows once more and the dec row again. 57(63:69) sts.

Cont in moss st until back measures 51(52:53)cm/ 20(20½:21)in from cast on edge, ending with a wrong side row.

Shape armholes

Cast off 4 sts at beg of next 2 rows. 49(55:61) sts.
Dec one st at each end of the next row and 2(3:4) foll alt rows. 43(47:51) sts.

Cont straight until back measures 76(78:80)cm/ 30(30¾:31½)in from cast on edge, ending with a wrong side row.

Shape shoulders

Cast off 6(7:7) sts at beg of next 2 rows and 7(7:8) sts at beg of foll 2 rows. 17(19:21) sts.
Cast off.

LEFT FRONT

With 9mm (US 13) needles, cast on 39(43:47) sts.
K 5 rows.
Change to 10mm (US 15) needles.
1st moss st row (right side) P1, [k1, p1] to last 6 sts, k6.
2nd moss st row K6, p1, [k1, p1] to end.
These 2 rows **form** the moss st with garter st border.
Work a further 16(18:20) rows.
Dec row (right side) Moss st 8, p3tog, moss st to last 6 sts, k6.
Work 29 rows.
Rep the last 30 rows once more and the dec row again. 33(37:41) sts.
Cont in patt until front measures 51(52:53)cm/20(20½:21)in from cast on edge, ending with a wrong side row.

Shape armhole

Next row Cast off 4 sts, patt to end. 29(33:37) sts.
Work 1 row.
Dec one st at armhole edge of the next row and 2(3:4) foll alt rows. 26(29:32) sts.
Cont straight until front measures 66(67:68)cm/ 26(26½:26¾)in from cast on edge, ending with a wrong side row.

Shape neck

Next row Patt to last 7(8:9) sts, turn and leave these 7(8:9) sts on a holder and cont on rem 19(21:23) sts.
Work 1 row.
Dec one st at neck edge on next row and 5(6:7) foll right side rows. 13(14:15) sts.
Cont straight until front measures same as Back to shoulder, ending at armhole edge.

Shape shoulder

Next row Cast off 6(7:7) sts, patt to end.
Work 1 row.
Cast off rem 7(7:8) sts.

RIGHT FRONT

With 9mm (US 13) needles, cast on 39(43:47) sts.
K 5 rows.
Change to 10mm (US 15) needles.
1st moss st row (right side) K6, p1, [k1, p1] to end.
2nd moss st row P1, [k1, p1] to last 6 sts, k6.
These 2 rows **form** the moss st with garter st border.
Work a further 16(18:20) rows.
Dec row (right side) K6, moss st to last 11 sts, p3tog, moss st 8.
Work 29 rows.
Rep the last 30 rows once more and the dec row again. 33(37:41) sts.
Cont in patt until front measures 51(52:53)cm/20(20½:21)in from cast on edge, ending with a right side row.

Shape armhole

Next row Cast off 4 sts, patt to end. 29(33:37) sts.
Dec one st at armhole edge of the next row and 2(3:4) foll alt rows. 26(29:32) sts.
Cont straight until front measures 66(67:68)cm/ 26(26½:26¾)in from cast on edge, ending with a wrong side row.

Shape neck

Next row Patt 7(8:9) sts, leave these 7(8:9) sts on a holder, patt to end.
Work 1 row.
Dec one st at neck edge of next row and 5(6:7) foll right side rows. 13(14:15) sts.
Cont straight until front measures same as Back to shoulder, ending at armhole edge.

Shape shoulder

Next row Cast off 6(7:7) sts, patt to end.
Work 1 row.
Cast off rem 7(7:8) sts.

SLEEVES

With 9mm (US 13) needles, cast on 29(33:41) sts.
K 5 rows.
Change to 10mm (US 15) needles.
Moss st row (right side) K1, [p1, k1] to end.
Work 6 rows.
Next row Inc in first st, moss st to end.

Rep the last 7 rows 9 times more. 39(43:51)sts.
Cont straight until sleeve measures 43(44:45)cm/
17(17¼:17¾)in from cast on edge, ending with
a wrong side row.

Shape sleeve top
Cast off 4 sts at beg of next 2 rows. 31(35:43) sts.
Dec one st at each end of the next row and 8(9:10)
foll alt rows. 13(15:21) sts.
Cast off 2 sts at beg of next 4(5:8) rows. 5 sts.
Cast off.

NECKBAND

Join shoulder seams.
With 9mm (US 13) needles, slip 7(8:9) sts from right front
holder onto a needle, pick up and k10(11:12) sts up
right front neck, 15(17:19) sts from back neck edge,
10(11:12) sts down left front neck, then k7(8:9) sts
from left front holder. 49(55:61) sts.
K 5 rows.
Buttonhole row K2, k2tog, yf, k to end.
K 4 rows.
Cast off.

TO MAKE UP

Join side and sleeve seams. Sew sleeves into armholes,
easing to fit. Join underarm seam. Sew on button.

T shape sweater

MEASUREMENTS

To fit bust

81–86	92–97	102–107	cm
32–34	36–38	40–42	in

FINISHED MEASUREMENTS

Bust

108	120	132	cm
42½	47¼	52	in

Length to shoulder

56	58	60	cm
22	22¾	23½	in

Sleeve length
20cm/8in for all sizes

MATERIALS

- 12(13:15) 50g balls of Debbie Bliss Como in Grey 02.
- Pair 10mm (US 15) knitting needles.

TENSION

10 sts and 15 rows to 10cm/4in square over st st
using 10mm (US 15) needles.

ABBREVIATIONS

Tw2R = k into front of 2nd st on left hand needle, then
k into front of 1st st and slip both sts off needle tog.

Also see page 22.

BACK and FRONT (both alike)

With 10mm (US 15) needles, cast on 54(62:66) sts.
1st row (wrong side) K2, [p2, k2] to end.
2nd row P2, [Tw2R, p2] to end.
Rep the last 2 rows for 12cm/4¾in, ending with
a wrong side row and inc 2(0:2) sts evenly across
last row. 56(62:68) sts
Beg with a k row, work in st st until back measures
30(31:32)cm/12(12¼:12½)in from cast on edge,
ending with a p row.
Shape sleeves
Cast on 5 sts at beg of next 4 rows. 76(82:88) sts.
Cont straight until back measures 52(54:56)cm/
20½(21¼:22)in from cast on edge, ending with a p row.

Back and Front

20 cm/8 in

56(58:60) cm
22(22¾:23½) in

30(31:32) cm
12(12¼:12½) in

56(62:68) cm
22(24½:26¾) in

Shape shoulders and front neck

Next row K32(35:38), turn and work on these sts only
for first side of neck.

Next row Cast off 3 sts, p to end.

Next row Cast off 8(9:10) sts, k to end.

Rep the last 2 rows once more.

Next row Cast off 2 sts, p to end.

Cast off rem 8(9:10) sts.

With right side facing, slip centre 12 sts onto a holder,
rejoin yarn to rem sts, cast off 3 sts, k to end.

Next row Cast off 8(9:10) sts, p to end.

Next row Cast off 3 sts, k to end.

Next row Cast off 8(9:10) sts, p to end.

Next row Cast off 2 sts, k to end.

Cast off rem 8(9:10) sts.

NECK EDGING

Join right shoulder seam.

With right side facing and 10mm (US 15) needles,
pick up and k8 sts, down side of neck, k across
12 sts on holder, pick up and k9 sts up side of neck;
rep from * once more. 58 sts.

1st row (wrong side) K2, [p2, k2] to end.

2nd row P2, [Tw2R, p2] to end.

Cast off in rib.

ARMBANDS

Join left shoulder and neck edging.

With right side facing and 10mm (US 15) needles,
pick up and k42(46:50) sts, evenly along armhole edge.

1st row (wrong side) K2, [p2, k2] to end.

2nd row P2, [Tw2R, p2] to end.

Rep the last 2 rows 6 times more.

Cast off in rib.

TO MAKE UP

Join side, sleeve and armband seams.

Mock rib jumper

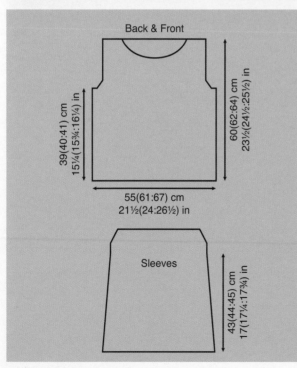

Back & Front

39(40:41) cm
15¼(15¾:16¼) in

60(62:64) cm
23½(24½:25½) in

55(61:67) cm
21½(24:26½) in

Sleeves

43(44:45) cm
17(17¼:17¾) in

MEASUREMENTS

To fit bust

81–86	92–97	102–107	cm
32–34	36–38	40–42	in

FINISHED MEASUREMENTS

Bust

106	118	130	cm
41¾	46½	51¼	in

Length to shoulder

60	62	64	cm
23½	24½	25½	in

Sleeve length

43	44	45	cm
17	17¼	17¾	in

MATERIALS

- 20(22:24) 50g balls of Debbie Bliss Como in Pink 11.
- Pair each 9mm (US 13) and 10mm (US 15) knitting needles.

TENSION

10 sts and 13 rows to 10cm/4in square over patt using 10mm (US 15) needles.

ABBREVIATIONS

See page 22.

NOTE

The sleeve decreases are staggered, working at the beg of every 13th row to avoid excess bulk when joining the sleeve seam.

BACK

With 9mm (US 13) needles, cast on 55(61:67) sts.
1st row (right side) K1, [p1, k1] to end.
2nd row P1, [k1, p1] to end.
Rep the last 2 rows once more.
Change to 10mm (US 15) needles.
1st row (right side) K to end.
2nd row P1, [k1, p1] to end.
These 2 rows **form** the patt and are repeated throughout.

Cont in patt until back measures 39(40:41)cm/
15¼(15¾:16¼)in from cast on edge, ending with
a wrong side row.
Shape armholes
Cast off 3 sts at beg of next 2 rows. 49(55:61) sts.
Next row (right side) Skpo, k to last 2 sts, k2tog.
Next row Patt to end.
Rep the last 2 rows 2(3:4) times more. 43(47:51) sts.
Cont straight until back measures 60(62:64)cm/
23½(24½:25½)in from cast on edge, ending with
a wrong side row.
Shape shoulders
Cast off 6(7:8) sts at beg of next 2 rows. 31(33:35) sts.
Cast off.

FRONT

With 9mm (US 13) needles, cast on 55(61:67) sts.
1st row (right side) P1, [k1, p1] to end.
2nd row K1, [p1, k1] to end.
Rep the last 2 rows once more.
Change to 10mm (US 15) needles.
1st row K to end.
2nd row K1, [p1, k1] to end.
These 2 rows **form** the patt and are repeated.
Cont in patt until front measures 39(40:41)cm/
15¼(15¾:16¼)in from cast on edge, ending with
a wrong side row.
Shape armholes
Cast off 3 sts at beg of next 2 rows. 49(55:61) sts.
Next row Skpo, k to last 2 sts, k2tog.
Next row Patt to end.
Rep the last 2 rows 2(3:4) times more. 43(47:51) sts.
Cont straight until front measures 52(54:56)cm/
20½(21¼:22)in from cast on edge, ending with
a wrong side row.
Shape neck
Next row Patt 17(18:19) sts, turn and work on
these sts only for first side of neck shaping.
Cast off 4 sts at beg of next row, 3 sts on foll
wrong side row, then 2 sts on next 2 wrong side rows.
6(7:8) sts.
Cont straight until front measures same as Back
to shoulder, ending at armhole edge.
Shape shoulder
Cast off.
With right side facing, slip centre 9(11:13) sts onto
a holder, rejoin yarn to rem sts, patt to end.
Complete to match first side, reversing shaping.

SLEEVES

With 10mm (US 15) needles, cast on 48(52:56) sts.
Rib row [K1, p1] to end.
Rep the last row 3 times more.
Next row (right side) K to end.
Next row [K1, p1] to end.
Dec row Work 2 tog, patt to end.
Work 12 rows.
Rep the last 13 rows twice more and the dec row again.
44(48:52) sts.
Cont straight until sleeve measures 43(44:45)cm/
17(17¼:17¾)in from cast on edge, ending with
a wrong side row.
Place markers at each end of last row.
Work a further 6 rows.
Shape sleeve top
Next row Skpo, patt to last 2 sts, k2tog.
Next row K to end.
Rep the last 2 rows 2(3:4) times more. 38(40:42) sts.
Cast off.

COLLAR

Join right shoulder seam.
With right side facing and 9mm (US 13) needles,
pick up and k21 sts down left front neck, k9(11:13) sts
from centre front holder, pick up and k21 sts up right
front neck, 31(33:35) sts from back neck. 82(86:90) sts.
Rib row [K1, p1] to end.
Rep the last row for 5cm/2in.
Change to 10mm (US 15) needles.
Work a further 20cm/8in.
Cast off in rib.

TO MAKE UP

Join left shoulder and collar seam, reversing seam on
last 20cm/8in of collar. Sew sleeves into armholes.
Join side and sleeve seams.

Ribbed scarf

SIZE

Approximately 137cm x 9cm/54in x 3½in.

MATERIALS

• Three 50gm balls of Debbie Bliss Como in Ecru 03.
• Pair 10mm (US 15) knitting needles.

TENSION

16 sts and 12 rows to 10cm/4in square over 1 x 1 rib,
using 10mm (US 15) needles.

ABBREVIATIONS

See page 22.

TO MAKE

With 10mm (US 15) needles, cast on 22 sts.
Beg with a k row, work 4 rows in st st.
1st row (right side) K1, [p2, k1] to end.
2nd row P1, [k2, p1] to end.
Rep these 2 rows 7 times more.
Dec row K1, [p2tog, k1] to end. 15sts.
Next row (wrong side) P1, [k1, p1] to end.
Next row K1, [p1, k1] to end.
Rep the last 2 rows for a further 105cm/41½in,
ending with a wrong side row.
Inc row K1, [pfb, k1] to end. 22 sts.
1st row P1, [k2, p1] to end.
2nd row K1, [p2, k1] to end.
Rep the last 2 rows 6 times more, then the 1st row again.
Work 4 rows in st st.
Cast off.

Reversible bag

SIZE

Approximately 36 x 24cm/14¼ x 9½in.

MATERIALS

- Three 50g balls of Debbie Bliss Como in each of Grey 02 (A) and Red 12 (B).
- Pair each 9 mm (US 13) and 10mm (US 15) knitting needles.

TENSION

- 9 sts and 18 rows to 10cm/4in square over moss st using 10mm (US 15) needles.

ABBREVIATIONS

See page 22.

TO MAKE

Inner bag
With 9mm (US 13) needles and B cast on 33 sts.
Beg with a k row, work in st st for 22cm/8¾in, ending with a p row.
Next row K10 sts, cast off 13 sts, k to end.
Next row P to end, casting on 13 sts over those cast off in previous row.
Work 3 rows.
Ridge row (wrong side) K to end.
Outer bag
Change to 10mm (US 15) needles and A.
K 1 row.
Moss st row K1, [p1, k1] to end.
Moss st 1 row.
Next row (right side) Moss st 10, cast off 13 sts, moss st to end.
Next row Moss st and cast on 13 sts over those cast off in previous row.
Cont in moss until outer bag measures 44cm/17¼in from colour change.
Next row (right side) Moss st 10, cast off 13 sts, moss st to end.
Next row Moss st and cast on 13 sts over those cast off in previous row.
Moss st 2 rows.
Inner bag
Change to 9mm (US 13) needles and B.
K 2 rows.
Beg with a k row, work 2 rows in st st.
Next row K10, cast off 13 sts, k to end.
Next row P, casting on 13 sts over those cast off in previous row.
Work a further 2 rows in st st, ending with a p row.
Cast off.

TO MAKE UP

Join cast on and cast off edges to form base of inner bag.
Join side seams of inner bag and side seams of outer bag.
Slip st inner bag to outer bag around handle openings.

Broken rib cardigan

MEASUREMENTS

To fit chest

86–92	97–102	107–112	117–122	cm
34–36	38–40	42–44	46–48	in

FINISHED MEASUREMENTS

Chest

114	127	140	152	cm
44¾	50	55¼	60	in

Length to shoulder

65	66	67	68	cm
25½	26	26½	26¾	in

Sleeve length

48cm/19in for all sizes

MATERIALS

- 20(22:24:26) 50g balls of Debbie Bliss Como in Grey 02.
- Pair each 9mm (US 13) and10mm (US 15) needles.
- 5 Buttons

TENSION

11 sts and 15 rows to 10cm/4in square over broken rib st using 10mm (US 15) needles.

ABBREVIATIONS

See page 22.

NOTE

The sleeve increases are staggered to avoid excess bulk when joining sleeve seams.

BACK

With 10mm (US 15) needles, cast on 63(69:75:81) sts.
1st row (right side) K1, [p1, k1] to end.
2nd row P1, [k1, p1] to end.
Rep the last 2 rows 5 times more.
Next row (right side) K1 tbl, [p1, k1tbl] to end.
Next row K to end.
These 2 rows **form** the broken rib st and are repeated.
Cont in patt until back measures 41cm/16¼in from cast on edge, ending with a wrong side row.

Back & Fronts

41 cm/16¼ in

65(66:67:68) cm
25½(26:26½:26¾) in

57.5(62.5:68:73.5) cm
22½(24½:26¾;29) in

Sleeves

48 cm/19 in

Shape armholes

Cast off 5 sts at beg of next 2 rows. 53(59:65:71) sts
Cont in patt until back measures 65(66:67:68)cm/
25½(26:26½:26¾)in from cast on edge, ending with
a wrong side row.

Shape shoulders

Cast off 9(10:11:12) sts at beg of next 4 rows.
Cast off rem 17(19:21:23) sts.

RIGHT FRONT

With 10mm (US 15) needles, cast on 36(40:44:48) sts.
1st row (right side) K3, p1, [k1, p1] to end.
2nd row [K1, p1] to last 2 sts, k2.
Rep the last 2 rows 5 times more.
Next row K2, [k1 tbl, p1] to end.
Next row K to end.
These 2 rows **form** the broken rib st with garter st
front edge.
Cont in patt until front measures 41cm/16¼in from
cast on edge, ending with a right side row.

Shape armhole

Next row Cast off 5 sts, patt to end. 31(35:39:43) sts
Cont in patt until front measures 65(66:67:68)cm/
25½(26:26½:26¾)in from cast on edge, ending with
a right side row.

Shape shoulder

Cast off 9(10:11:12) sts at beg of next row and foll
wrong side row. 13(15:17:19) sts.

Shape collar

Next 2 rows Patt 7(8:9:10), turn and k to end.
Work 2 rows.
Rep the last 4 rows 7(8:8:9) times more.
Cast off.
Mark position for 5 buttons, the first 4cm/1½in from
cast on edge, the fifth 40cm/15¾in from cast on edge,
with the rem 3 spaced evenly between.

LEFT FRONT

1st buttonhole row (right side) Patt to last 6 sts,
k2tog, y2rn, skpo, k2.
2nd buttonhole row K3, k into front and back of y2rn,
k to end.
With 10mm (US 15) needles, cast on 36(40:44:48) sts.
1st row (right side) P1, [k1, p1] to last 3 sts, k3.
2nd row K2, [p1, k1] to end.
Rep the last 2 rows 5 times more, working buttonhole
to match marker.

Next row [P1, k1tbl] to last 2 sts, k2.
Next row K to end.
These 2 rows **form** the broken rib st with garter st edging.
Cont in patt, working rem buttonholes to match markers,
until front measures 41cm/16¼in from cast on edge,
ending with a wrong side row.

Shape armhole

Next row Cast off 5 sts, patt to end. 31(35:39:43) sts
Cont in patt until front measures 65(66:67:68)cm/
25½(26:26½:26¾)in from cast on edge, ending with
a wrong side row.

Shape shoulder

Cast off 9(10:11:12) sts at beg of next row and foll
right side row. 13(15:17:19) sts.

Shape collar

Next 2 rows K7(8:9:10), turn and patt to end.
Work 2 rows.
Rep the last 4 rows 7(8:8:9) times more.
Cast off.

SLEEVES

With 9mm (US 13) needles, cast on 32(34:36:38) sts.
1st row [K1, p1] to end.
Rep the last row 11 times more.
Change to 10mm (US 15) needles.
Next row [K1tbl, p1] to end.
Next row K to end.
Next row Inc in first st, patt to end.
Patt 3 rows.
Next row Patt to last st, inc in last st.
Patt 3 rows.
Rep the last 8 rows 6 times more. 46(48:50:52) sts.
Work straight until sleeve measures 48cm/19in from
cast on edge, ending with a wrong side row.
Place a marker at each end of last row.
Work a further 6 rows.

Shape sleeve top

Cast off 3 sts at beg of next 12 rows.
Cast off 10(12:14:16) sts.

TO MAKE UP

Join shoulder seams. Join cast off edges of collar
together. Sew row ends of collar to back neck edge.
Join side and sleeve seams. Sew sleeves into armholes,
easing to fit and with row ends above markers sewn to
sts cast off at underarm. Sew on buttons.

Tank top

Back and Front

35(36:36:37) cm
13¾(14¼:14¼:14½) in

47(52:57:62) cm
18½(20½:22½:24½) in

56(58:60:62) cm
22(22¾:23½:24½) in

MEASUREMENTS

To fit bust

| 81–86 | 92–97 | 102–107 | 112–117 | cm |
| 32–34 | 36–38 | 40–42 | 44–46 | in |

FINISHED MEASUREMENTS

Bust

| 92 | 102 | 112 | 122 | cm |
| 36 | 40 | 44 | 48 | in |

Length to shoulder

| 56 | 58 | 60 | 62 | cm |
| 22 | 22¾ | 23½ | 24½ | in |

MATERIALS

- 9(10:11:12) 50g balls of Debbie Bliss Como in Chocolate 015.
- Pair 10mm (US 15) knitting needles.

TENSION

10 sts and 15 rows to 10cm/4in square over patt using 10mm (US 15) needles.

ABBREVIATIONS

See page 22.

BACK and FRONT (both alike)

With 10mm (US 15) needles cast on 47(52:57:62) sts.
1st row (right side) K to end.
2nd row K2, [p3, k2] to end.
These 2 rows **form** the patt and are repeated throughout.
Cont in patt until back measures 51(53:55:57)cm/ 20(21:21¾:22½)in from cast on edge, ending with a wrong side row.
Shape neck
Next row (right side) K16(18:20:22), turn and work on these sts only for first side of neck shaping.
Next row Sl 1, patt to end.
Next row K13(14:15:16), turn.
Next row Sl 1, patt to end.
Next row K10(10:11:12), turn.
Next row Sl 1, patt to end.
Shape shoulder
Next row (right side) K to end.

Next row Patt 16(18:20:22), turn and work on these sts for second side of neck shaping.
Next row Sl 1, k to end.
Next row Patt 13(14:15:16), turn.
Next row Sl 1, k to end.
Next row Patt 10(10:11:12), turn.
Next row Sl 1, k to end.
Cast off all 47(52:57:62) sts.

TO MAKE UP

Join 7(8:9:10) sts for shoulder seams. Join side seams, leaving 21(22:24:25)cm/8¼(8¾:9½:10)in open for armhole.

Striped sweater

MEASUREMENTS

To fit chest

92–97	102–107	112–117 cm
36–38	40–42	44–46 in

FINISHED MEASUREMENTS

Chest

120	132	144	cm
47¼	52	57	in

Length to shoulder

62	63	64	cm
24½	25	25½	in

Sleeve length

48cm/19in for all sizes

MATERIALS

- 9(10:11) 50g balls Debbie Bliss Como in each of Chocolate 15 (A) and Red 12 (B).
- Pair each 9mm (US 13) and 10mm (US 15) knitting needles.

TENSION

10 sts and 15 rows to 10cm/4in square over st st using 10mm (US 15) needles.

ABBREVIATIONS

See page 22.

BACK

With 10mm (US 15) needles and A, cast on 62(66:74) sts.
1st row K2, [p2, k2] to end.
2nd row P2, [k2, p2] to end.
Rep the last 2 rows for 3(4:5) times more, inc 0(2:0) sts across last row. 62(68:74) sts.
Beg with a k row, work in st st stripes of 6 rows B and 6 rows A until 84 rows in stripe patt have been worked.
Shape shoulders
With B, cast off 21(23:25) sts at beg of next 2 rows.
Leave rem 20(22:24) sts on a holder.

FRONT

Work as given for Back until 72 rows in stripe patt have been worked.

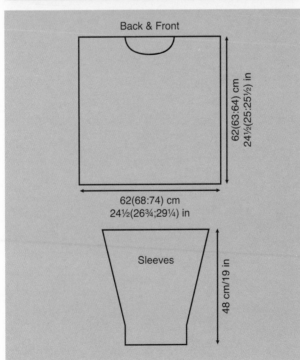

Back & Front

62(63:64) cm
24½(25:25½) in

62(68:74) cm
24½(26¾;29¼) in

Sleeves

48 cm/19 in

Shape neck

Keeping stripe patt correct, work as follows:

Next row (right side) K22(24:26), k2tog, k2, turn and work on these sts only for first side of neck shaping.

P one row.

Next row K to last 4 sts, k2tog, k2.

Next row P to end.

Rep the last 2 rows 3 times more. 21(23:25) sts.

Work 2 more rows.

Cast off.

With right side facing, slip centre 10(12:14) sts onto a holder, rejoin yarn to rem sts, k2, skpo, k to end.

Complete to match first side, reversing shaping.

SLEEVES

With 9mm (US 13) needles and A, cast on 26(30:34) sts.

Work 12 rows in rib as given for Back.

Change to 10mm (US 15) needles.

Beg with a k row, work in st st stripes of 6 rows B and 6 rows A.

Work 2 rows.

Inc row K3, m1, k to last 3 sts, m1, k3.

Work 5 rows.

Rep the last 6 rows 8 times and the inc row again. 46(50:54) sts.

Work 3 rows, so ending with 6 rows in A.

Cast off.

NECKBAND

Join right shoulder seam.

With right side facing, 9mm (US 13) needle and B, pick up and k12 sts down left side of front neck, k across 10(12:14) sts from centre front, pick up and k12 sts up right side of front neck, k across 20(22:24) sts from back neck holder. 54(58:62) sts.

1st row P2, [k2, p2] to end.

2nd row K2, [p2, k2] to end.

Rep the last 2 rows 3 times more and the 1st row again.

Cast off in rib.

TO MAKE UP

Join left shoulder and neckband seam. With centre of cast off edge of sleeve to shoulder, sew on sleeves. Join side and sleeve seams.

Moss stitch scarf

SIZE

Approx 235cm/93in long and 20cm/8in wide.

MATERIALS

• Nine 50gm balls of Debbie Bliss Como in Denim 07.
• Pair of 20mm (US 36) knitting needles.

TENSION

5.5 sts and 8 rows to 10cm/4in square over moss st using 20mm (US 36) needles and double yarn.

ABBREVIATIONS

See page 22.

TO MAKE

With two strands of yarn held together and 20mm (US 36) needles, cast on 11 sts.
Moss st row K1, [p1, k1] to end.
Rep this row until work measures approximately 235cm/93in from cast on edge or until the last ball of yarn is almost finished, leaving just enough yarn to work the cast off row.
Cast off.

Daisy stitch hat

To fit an average sized adult head.

FINISHED MEASUREMENTS

Around band (unstretched) 52cm/20½in.
Around crown 71cm/28in.

MATERIALS

- Four 50g balls of Debbie Bliss Como in Denim 07.
- Pair each of 5mm (US 8) and 10mm (US 15) knitting needles.

TENSION

11 sts and 12 rows to 10cm/4in square over daisy stitch patt using 10mm (US 15) needles.

ABBREVIATIONS

See page 22.

TO MAKE

Band
With 5mm (US 8) needles, cast on 81 sts.
1st row (right side) P1, [k1, p1] to end.
2nd row K1, [p1, k1] to end.
These 2 rows **form** rib.
Rib 4 more rows.

Crown
Change to 10mm (US 15) needles.
1st row (right side) K.
2nd row K1, [p3tog but do not drop sts from left needle, yo, p same 3 sts tog and drop off left needle, k1] to end.
3rd row K.
4th row K1, p1, k1, [p3tog but do not drop sts from left needle, yo, p same 3 sts tog and drop off left needle, k1] to last 2 sts, p1, k1.
These 4 rows **form** daisy stitch patt and are repeated.

Cont in patt and work 21 more rows, so ending with a 1st patt row.

Shape top
1st row (wrong side) K1, [p3tog, k1] to end. 41 sts.
2nd row K.
3rd row K1, [p3tog but do not drop sts from left needle, yo, p same 3 sts tog and drop off left needle, k1] to end.
4th row K.
5th row K3tog, [p3tog, k1] to last 6 sts, p3tog, k3tog. 19 sts.
6th row [K2tog] 9 times, k1. 10 sts.
7th row K1, [p2tog] 4 times, k1. 6 sts.
Leaving a long end, cut yarn, thread through rem 6 sts, draw up and secure.
Join seam.

Distributors

For stockists of Debbie Bliss yarns please contact:

UK & WORLDWIDE DISTRIBUTORS

Designer Yarns Ltd

Units 8–10 Newbridge Industrial Estate
Pitt Street, Keighley
West Yorkshire BD21 4PQ
UNITED KINGDOM

T +44 (0)1535 664222
F +44 (0)1535 664333
E alex@designeryarns.uk.com
www.designeryarns.uk.com

USA

Knitting Fever Inc.

315 Bayview Avenue
Amityville,
NY 11701
USA

T +1 516 546 3600
F +1 516 546 6871
www.knittingfever.com

CANADA

Diamond Yarns Ltd

155 Martin Ross Avenue Unit 3
Toronto
Ontario M3J 2L9
CANADA

T +1 416 736 6111
F +1 416 736 6112
www.diamondyarn.com

DENMARK

Fancy Knit

Hovedvejen 71
8586 Oerum Djurs
Ramten
DENMARK

T +45 59 4621 89
E roenneburg@mail.dk

MEXICO

Estambres Crochet SA de CV

Aaron Saenz 1891-7
Col. Santa Maria
Monterrey
N.L. 64650
MEXICO

T +52 81 8335 3870
E abremer@redmundial.com.mx

BELGIUM/HOLLAND

Pavan

Thomas Van Theemsche
Meerlaanstraat 73
9860 Balegem (Oostrezele)
BELGIUM

T +32 (0) 9 221 85 94
F +32 (0) 9 221 56 62
E pavan@pandora.be

ICELAND

Storkurinn ehf

Laugavegi 59
101 Reykjavík
ICELAND

T +354 551 8258
F +354 562 8252
E storkurinn@simnet.is

GERMANY/AUSTRIA/ SWITZERLAND/LUXEMBOURG

Designer Yarns (Deutschland) GmbH

Sachsstrasse 30
D-50259 Pulheim-Brauweiler
GERMANY

T +49 (0) 2234 205453
F +49 (0) 2234 205456
E info@designeryarns.de
www.designeryarns.de

FRANCE

Elle Tricote

8 Rue du Coq, La Petite France
67000 Strasbourg
FRANCE

T +33 (0) 388 230313
F +33 (0) 8823 0169
www.elletricote.com

SPAIN

Oyambre Needlework SL

Balmes, 200 At.4
08006 Barcelona
SPAIN

T +34 (0) 93 487 26 72
F +34 (0) 93 218 6694
E info@oyambreonline.com

SWEDEN

Nysta garn och textil

Luntmakargatan 50
S-113 58 Stockholm
SWEDEN

T +46 (0) 8 612 0330
E nina@nysta.se
www.nysta.se

AUSTRALIA/NEW ZEALAND

Prestige Yarns Pty Ltd

P O Box 39
Bulli NSW 2516
AUSTRALIA

T +61 02 4285 6669
E info@prestigeyarns.com
www.prestigeyarns.com

FINLAND

Duo Design

Hämeentie 26
00530 Helsinki
FINLAND

T +358 50,346 0575
E maria.hellbom@priima.net
www.duodesign.fi

BRAZIL

Quatro Estacoes Com Las Linhas e Acessorios Ltda

Av. Das Nacoes Unidas
12551-9 Andar
Cep 04578-000 Sao Paulo
BRAZIL

T +55 11 3443 7736
E cristina@4estacoeslas.com.br

For more information on all my
books and yarns, please visit:
www.debbieblissonline.com

Acknowledgements

This book would not have been possible without the incredible participation of the following:

Penny Hill whose pattern compiling and organisational skills have been invaluable.

Rosy Tucker for her technical expertise and pattern checking.

Mia Pejcinovic for the great styling.

Firyals for the lovely hair and make up.

Stella Smith for the second check and schematics.

Teresa Conway for the lovely moss stitch scarf.

The brilliant models, Alice and her brother Andrew.

David Watt, John Cashell and all at Designer Yarns for their tremendous support and Sion Elalouf for making it all happen.

Anna at MARC&ANNA for the lovely design of the booklet.

The wonderful knitters: Cynthia Brent, Pat Church, Jacqui Dunt, Maisie Lawrence and Frances Wallace.

Como

The Big Easy... 16 knits and
accessories for men and women